BREAKING

INTO

BRILLIANCE

D1092030

An Awakening of Creative Consciousness

Have a wonderful journey
Love Lynn Singer

Art & text by Lynn Singer

FORWARD

Lynn Singer has written a brave book. Breaking into Brilliance is her story of transformation, but she has paid it forward so it can become your story of transformation.

Packed with beautiful original artwork, stories, dreams and exercises, Lynn becomes the gentle guide that illuminates your inner brilliance and your true nature, allowing your true self to shine through. This book can help you unlock the answers to these questions and many more: What are my gifts? What did I come to earth to do? What can I do to help me live my best life now?

This book has become a friend to me, and I hope it will become a friend to you.

Susan Lander
Author, "Conversations with History"